THREE RIVERS REGIONAL LIBRARY SYSTEM

3 3400 50051 0857

Three Rivers Regional
Library System
Gilchrist County
Public Library
P.O. Box 128
Trenton, FL 32693

D1401948

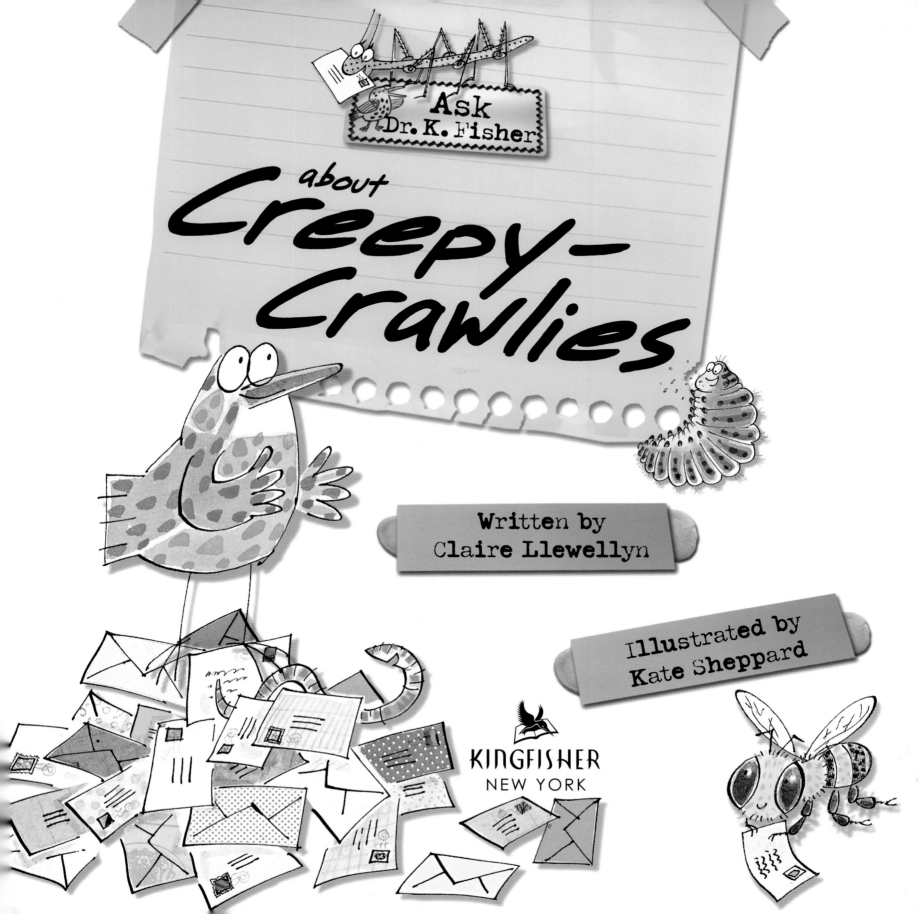

Ask Dr. K. Fisher

about Creepy-Crawlies

Written by
Claire Llewellyn

Illustrated by
Kate Sheppard

KINGFISHER
NEW YORK

Claire

Kate

Consultant: David Burnie

Copyright © 2008 by Macmillan Publishers Ltd.
Text and concept © 2008 by Claire Llewellyn
KINGFISHER
Published in the United States by Kingfisher, an imprint of Henry Holt
and Company LLC, 175 Fifth Avenue, New York, New York 10010.
First published in Great Britain by Kingfisher Publications plc, an imprint
of Macmillan Children's Books, London.
All rights reserved
Distributed in Canada by H. B. Fenn and Company Ltd.

Library of Congress Cataloging-in-Publication Data
has been applied for.

ISBN: 978-0-7534-6180-8

Kingfisher books are available for special promotions and premiums.
For details contact: Director of Special Markets, Holtzbrinck Publishers.

First American edition August 2008
Printed in China
10 9 8 7 6 5 4 3 2 1
1TR/0508/TECH/SCHOY/157MA/C

For Samuel, with love—C. L.
For William—K. S.

Kingfisher

Henry Holt and Company

175 Fifth Avenue

New York, NY 10010

Ask Dr. K. Fisher about . . .

Here's a scorpion anxious to sting

Dogs beware!

Dear Dr. K. Fisher,

I'm a male scorpion, and I live in the desert. I've always been self-conscious about being so small (I'm only a few inches long from tip to tail). The other day a friend told me that, tiny or not, the stinger I have in my tail could kill a dog in seven minutes flat. Is this true or was he just being kind? Maybe I should test it out. If so, where can I get a dog? Around here, they are hard to find.

Small but Hopeful,
in the Sahara Desert

dog

scorpion

4

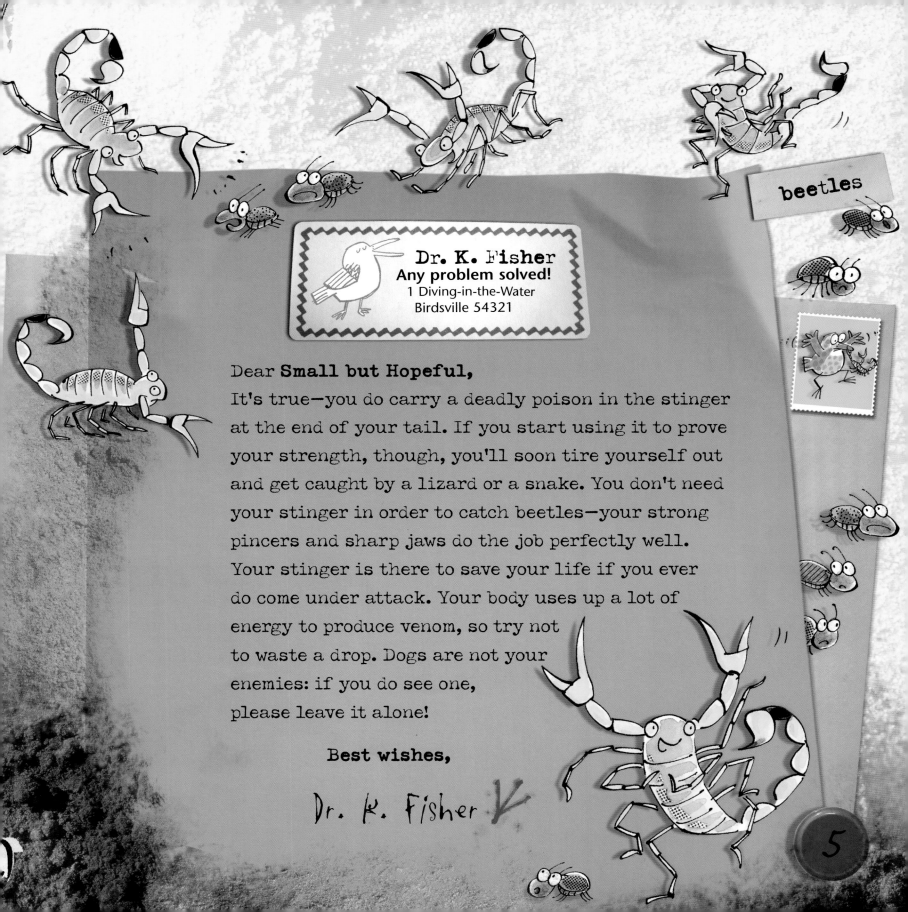

Dr. K. Fisher
Any problem solved!
1 Diving-in-the-Water
Birdsville 54321

beetles

Dear **Small but Hopeful,**

It's true—you do carry a deadly poison in the stinger at the end of your tail. If you start using it to prove your strength, though, you'll soon tire yourself out and get caught by a lizard or a snake. You don't need your stinger in order to catch beetles—your strong pincers and sharp jaws do the job perfectly well. Your stinger is there to save your life if you ever do come under attack. Your body uses up a lot of energy to produce venom, so try not to waste a drop. Dogs are not your enemies: if you do see one, please leave it alone!

Best wishes,

Dr. K. Fisher

Here's an unhappy earthworm

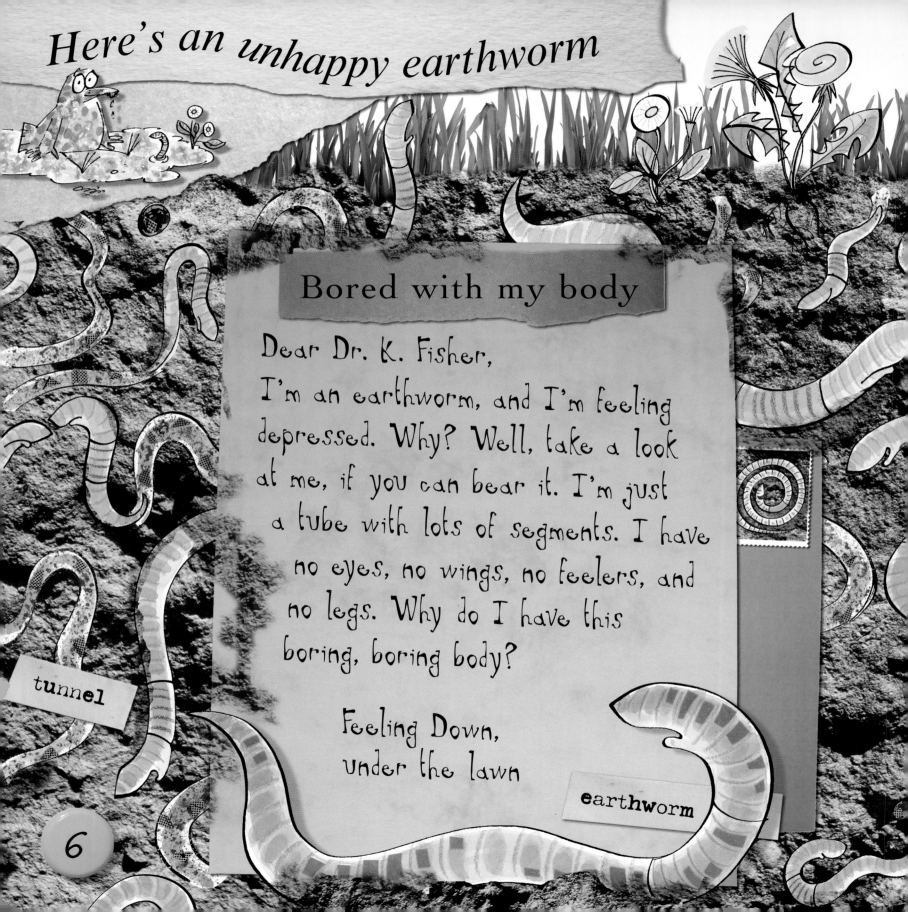

Bored with my body

Dear Dr. K. Fisher,

I'm an earthworm, and I'm feeling depressed. Why? Well, take a look at me, if you can bear it. I'm just a tube with lots of segments. I have no eyes, no wings, no feelers, and no legs. Why do I have this boring, boring body?

Feeling Down,
under the lawn

tunnel

earthworm

bird

Dr. K. Fisher
Any problem solved!
1 Diving-in-the-Water
Birdsville 54321

Dear **Feeling Down,**

You have the perfect body for underground life. Your long, smooth shape helps you burrow through the soil, while your body segments contain powerful muscles that pull and push you along. They also help you hold on tight when birds try to tug you up from the ground. Cheer up! You worms are important animals. As you feed on mud and rotting plants, your body breaks them down into fine, fertile soil. And your tunnels let in plenty of oxygen and water, making the soil the perfect place for healthy plants to grow.

Yours truly,

Dr. K. Fisher

Turn the page for **more** about creepy-crawly bodies . . .

7

Dr. K. Fisher's Guide to Creepy-Crawly Bodies

There are many different groups of creepy-crawlies, including snails, worms, millipedes, spiders, and insects. Each group has its own special body plan.

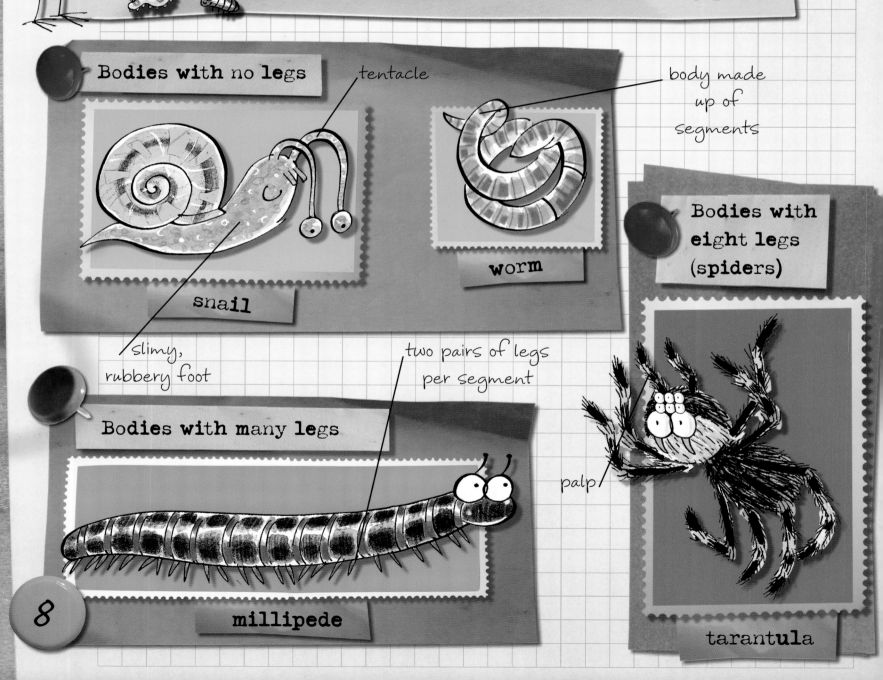

Bodies with no legs

tentacle

body made up of segments

snail

worm

slimy, rubbery foot

two pairs of legs per segment

Bodies with many legs

millipede

Bodies with eight legs (spiders)

palp

tarantula

Bodies with **six legs** and **made up of**
head, thorax, and **abdomen** (insects)

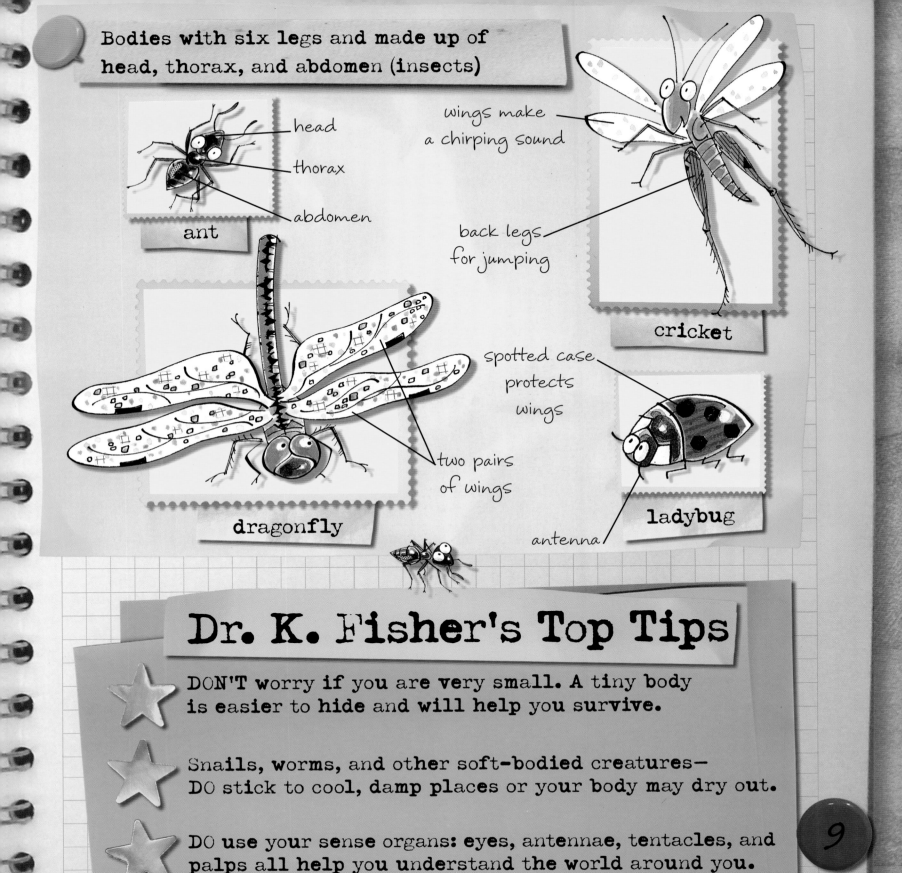

head

thorax

abdomen

ant

wings make
a chirping sound

back legs
for jumping

cricket

two pairs
of wings

dragonfly

spotted case
protects
wings

ladybug

antenna

Dr. K. Fisher's Top Tips

⭐ **DON'T** worry if you are **very small. A tiny body**
is easier to hide and **will help you survive.**

⭐ Snails, **worms,** and other soft-bodied creatures—
DO stick to **cool, damp places** or your body **may dry out.**

⭐ **DO use** your sense organs: **eyes,** antennae, **tentacles,** and
palps all help **you understand** the **world** around you.

Turn off the light!

Dear Dr. K. Fisher,

I'm a female glowworm, and I have an embarrassing problem. I just can't stop blushing. Whenever I'm out on warm summer nights, my abdomen flashes with a bright yellow glow. I can't seem to control it! I think the moths and crickets are laughing at me. Please, please, please help me cure this horrible habit.

Bothered by Blushes,
at twilight

moth

cricket

female glowworm

10

Dr. K. Fisher
Any problem solved!
1 Diving-in-the-Water
Birdsville 54321

Dear **Bothered by Blushes,**

Don't be embarrassed any longer. You are an adult now, and it's time to look for a partner—a male glowworm who can father your young. Nocturnal (nighttime) animals like glowworms can have problems finding mates in the dark. So you use a special signal: your body produces a bright yellow light that flashes on and off. If a male spots your light in the darkness, he will fly down to say hello. I'm sure you'll know if he's Mr. Right.

Good luck!

Dr. K. Fisher

male glowworm

flashing female glowworm

11

A need for speed!

THE WOODLAND
AUG. 23RD
MAIL

Dear Dr. K. Fisher,
I'm a millipede, and I'm
feeling humiliated. My cousin's
an arrogant centipede, and last
week I challenged him to a race.
(I have more legs than him,
so I thought I'd win.) But
he passed me right away!
Now he wants a rematch,
and I'm bound to lose. Help!
Feel like a Loser,
in the leaves

Dr. K. Fisher

1 Diving-in-the-Water

Birdsville 54321

millipede

Finish Line

centipede

12

centipede chasing
his lunch

Dr. K. Fisher
Any problem solved!
1 Diving-in-the-Water
Birdsville 54321

Dear **Feel like a Loser,**

Your centipede cousin needs his speed. He's a carnivore and has to catch other creepy-crawlies to eat. You millipedes are herbivores, munching mostly on dead leaves that can't run away. Yes, you have more legs than your cousin. Millipedes have four legs on each segment of their bodies, while centipedes have only two on each segment. But they wiggle fast over the ground, while you crawl slowly. Avoid another race—just tell him that you're too busy. Try not to annoy him, though, as he has sharp jaws and poisonous fangs. If he gets nasty, curl up until he goes away.

Best wishes,

Dr. K. Fisher

millipede enjoying
an easy meal

13

Battle of the bulge

Dear Dr. K. Fisher,

I'm a caterpillar, and I'm worried about myself. My body has grown so much and my skin's so tight that I feel like it's going to burst. Could my eating habits be the problem? I feed all day long on juicy green leaves— they are surprisingly delicious— and I just can't stop. Do you think the leaves are to blame?

Always Hungry,

in the Leaves

14

caterpillar about to burst

Dr. K. Fisher
Any problem solved!
1 Diving-in-the-Water
Birdsville 54321

butterfly

Dear **Always Hungry,**
What you describe is perfectly normal. Like many creepy-crawlies, you have a tough outer skin called an exoskeleton that protects your body. As you eat and grow, this skin regularly splits, and underneath there is new skin in a larger size. The fifth time this process happens, you change into a pupa, a new, exciting stage in your life cycle when your body develops into its adult form. After two weeks, you will crawl out as a butterfly. You'll feed from flowers instead of leaves and you'll have a wonderful set of wings.

Good luck!

Dr. K. Fisher

Almost there!

egg

pupa

Turn the page for **more about insect wings . . .**

caterpillar

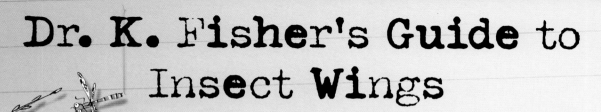

Dr. K. Fisher's Guide to Insect Wings

Most adult insects have wings and can fly. Flying helps them hunt, find mates, and escape from danger. The different types of wings provide each of the insects on these pages with the perfect flying equipment.

A **butterfly** has two pairs of wings. They shimmer beautifully in the sunlight—perfect for attracting a **mate!**

Wasps have two pairs of small, delicate wings. They are perfect for fast flying.

wasp

morpho butterfly

Dragonflies are expert fliers, with two pairs of strong wings. They can hover, shoot up or down, or even fly backward.

This beetle has fragile flying wings. When it's on the ground, it tucks them away underneath its hard wing cases.

Flies have only one pair of wings. These wings beat so fast that they buzz.

atlas beetle

fly

dragonfly

Dr. K. Fisher's Top Tips

DO take care of your wings. They are very important to you but are also fragile and easily damaged.

DO find a good place to take off into the air. The top of a flower stalk makes a great launch site.

DON'T forget to eat frequently. It takes a lot of energy to fly.

Here's a hover fly with an eating problem

A fine mess

Dear Dr. K. Fisher,

I'm a male hover fly, and I pride myself on my good manners. So I'm troubled by a delicate feeding problem. Every time I suck nectar from a flower, I get covered in a sticky yellow dust. It gets all over me, from my feelers to my feet. How can I learn to eat more neatly?

Messy Eater,
in the meadow

flowers

hover fly

Dr. K. Fisher
Any problem solved!
1 Diving-in-the-Water
Birdsville 54321

Dear **Messy Eater,**

Don't worry—it's impossible for you to drink nectar without picking up pollen, too. Pollen (that's the name for the sticky yellow dust) helps plants make seeds, but first it must be moved from flower to flower. Plants can't move the pollen themselves, so most get insects to do it for them. As you feed, you collect the pollen, which rubs off when you visit the next flower. You are doing an important job: every time you pollinate a flower, you are helping new seeds grow.

Best wishes,

Dr. K. Fisher

helpful hover fly

other pollinating insects at work

19

Here's a worried stick insect

Oh brother!

Dear Dr. K. Fisher,
I'm a male stick insect, and I'm concerned about my brother. A week ago, we were sitting side by side, but when I turned around, he'd disappeared, and I haven't seen him since. It's tough finding him on this bush. Whenever I think I've spotted him, "he" turns out to be a twig. There are geckos and birds around here, and I'm worried that they'll catch the little guy. What do you think I should do?

Fretting about Family,
in the forest

stick insect

Dr. K. Fisher
Any problem solved!
1 Diving-in-the-Water
Birdsville 54321

Dear **Fretting about Family,**
Try not to worry about your brother. Stick insects have long, brown, slender bodies that blend in perfectly against branches and twigs and are almost impossible to spot. This camouflage is such an amazing defense that predators are unlikely to catch your brother. Unfortunately, this means that you are also unlikely to find him, unless you're very lucky and patient and you manage to catch him while he's actually moving.

Yours sincerely,

Dr. K. Fisher

golden gecko
(**predator!**)

Found **him!**

Turn the page for **more** about insect disguises . . .

Dr. K. Fisher's Guide to Insect Disguises

Insects are the masters of disguise. All of the insects on these pages have developed camouflage in order to blend in with their surroundings. This allows them to hide from predators or prey. They're all difficult to spot!

Leaf insect

Habitat: Tropical rainforests

Camouflage: Body shape and color make it look like a leaf.

How it works: Predators do not recognize the insect as food and leave it alone.

Bonus: If grabbed, a leaf insect can shed a leg and make a quick escape.

Spotted? I spotted him last week.

Orchid mantis

Habitat: Tropical rainforests

Camouflage: Pink body and petal-shaped legs blend in against orchid flowers.

How it works: Mantis hides on a flower, waiting to gobble up insects that feed there.

Bonus: Its clever camouflage keeps it hidden from predators, too.

Spotted? What a neat disguise!

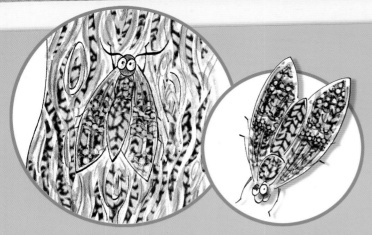

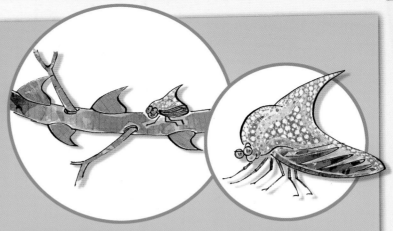

Pine hawk moth

Habitat: Pine forests

Camouflage: Dull, blotchy wings that blend in with tree bark.

How it works: Allows it to rest on a tree in the daytime without being spotted.

Bonus: As a caterpillar, the hawk moth has a different disguise—as a pine needle.

Spotted? I **haven't seen this one yet.**

Thorn bug

Habitat: The stems of young tropical trees

Camouflage: Hard, triangular, pointed body that looks like a thorn.

How it works: Predators don't see it. They mistake it for part of a plant.

Bonus: Predators dislike the thorn bug's hard, spiky body, which is painful to eat.

Spotted? ✓ Ouch—he's sharp!

Dr. K. Fisher's Top Tips

 DON'T move an inch! Camouflage works only if you stay **very still.**

 **DON'T feed** during the daytime when predators can see you. It's **much** safer to eat at night.

Remember, eggs and droppings can give you away. DON'T leave them near your hiding place.

Here's a worn-out spider

What an effort!

squirrel monkey
(web destroyer!)

Dear Dr. K. Fisher,

I'm a female spider, and I'm feeling fed up. Early every morning, I make a web. Spinning silk is very tricky, and I work hard to get it right. But most days, my web ends up in tatters— animals walk or fly into it or it gets spoiled by the wind and rain. I end up having to destroy it myself and start all over again the next day. Surely there are easier ways to catch a meal.

Wasting a Lifetime, on the web

golden silk
orb-web spider

24

Dr. K. Fisher
Any problem solved!
1 Diving-in-the-Water
Birdsville 54321

Dear **Wasting a Lifetime,**
A sticky web is a great way to catch flying insects, and is building one *really* so hard? A web like yours takes only around one hour to build. It's true that you do have to renew it most days, but at least you can eat the old one and recycle the precious silk. There ARE other ways of catching a meal. Some spiders build traps and ambush their prey; others simply jump on it, but they have better eyesight than you. Spinning a web is a real talent—I would stick with it if I were you.

Best wishes,

Dr. K. Fisher

Here's a hard-working honeybee

Give me a break!

Dear Dr. K. Fisher,

I'm a female honeybee, and all I ever do is work, work, work. We girls never stop: we have to clean the nest, care for the eggs, larvae, and pupae, search for nectar, make honey, AND feed the queen. Meanwhile, she and the drones, the lazy male bees, never do a thing. I'm tired of being a slave. What do you think I should do?

Hot and Bothered,
in the nest

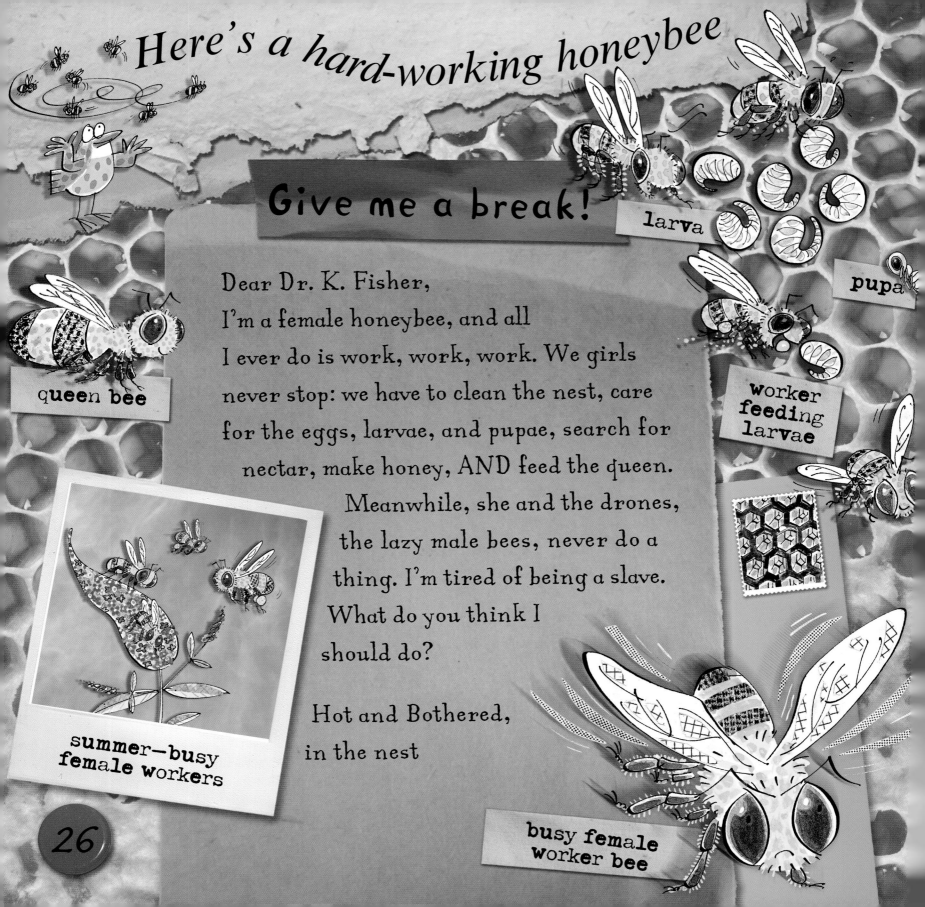

queen bee

summer–busy female workers

larva

pupa

worker feeding larvae

busy female worker bee

26

winter— goodbye, guys!

Dr. K. Fisher
Any problem solved!
1 Diving-in-the-Water
Birdsville 54321

Dear **Hot and Bothered,**

Honeybees live in a colony—a huge team that sticks together to build a home, find food, fend off enemies, and care for the young. You and the other female bees work hard all summer long, inside the nest and out. The queen, poor thing, lays eggs all day. It's true that the drones, or male bees, have an easy life right now, but they will be kicked out of the nest during the winter to shiver in the cold. Then the females will dine on delicious honey and enjoy a well-deserved break.

Good luck!

Dr. K. Fisher

winter—females
taking a break!

Turn the page for **more** about insect colonies . . .

Dr. K. Fisher's Guide to Insect Colonies

Some insects **live** in groups called colonies. In a colony, all of the insects work as a **team** to **build** and care for the nest. **The** ants on **these pages** are part of one colony. **Each** ant **has** a **special** job to do.

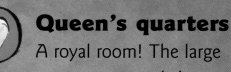

Queen's quarters
A royal room! The large queen ant spends her whole life laying eggs.

Boys-only den
Male ants mate with the queen but spend most of their time resting.

Construction site
Workers hollow out the nest and build new tunnels.

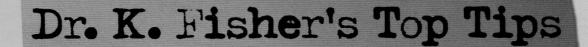

Dr. K. Fisher's Top Tips

DON'T let your colony get too crowded. If it does, some of you should fly away in a swarm and start a new colony.

DO build your nest **where predators won't easily find it**—in a cave, a hollow tree, or under the ground.

DO build your nest **with the right materials:** wax for bees, chewed-up wood for wasps, and soil for ants.

Nursery 1
Workers (females) take the new eggs to a safe place to hatch.

Nursery 2
Workers are busy feeding the larvae.

Nursery 3
Workers make sure that the pupae are safe and warm.

Glossary

abdomen
The back part of a creepy-crawly's body.

antenna
A feeler that picks up scents in the air and helps creepy-crawlies move around.

camouflage
A shape, color, or pattern that helps an animal hide.

carnivore
A meat-eating animal.

colony
A large group of animals that live together.

disguise
A shape, color, or pattern that makes a creepy-crawly look like something else so that it can escape from danger.

drone
A male honeybee.

fertile
Something that is good and rich—like soil where many plants can grow.

fragile
Easily ruined.

herbivore
A plant-eating animal.

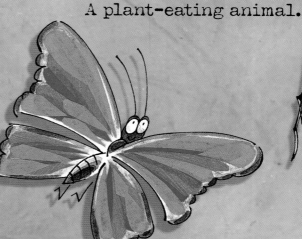

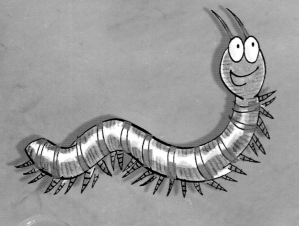

insect
A type of creepy-crawly that has six legs.

larva
The second stage in an insect's life cycle after it has hatched from an egg.

30

nectar
The sugary juice inside flowers.

nocturnal
Active at night.

oxygen
A gas found in air that all animals need to breathe in order to survive.

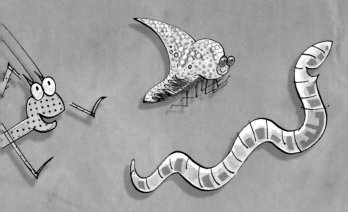

palp
A special feeler near a creepy-crawly's jaws that helps it feel and taste its food.

pollen
A yellow dust made by flowers. When it is spread to the same type of flowers, they can make seeds.

pollinate
To move pollen from one flower to another of the same type.

predator
An animal that hunts other animals (prey) for food.

prey
An animal that is eaten by other animals (predators).

pupa
The stage in an insect's life cycle when it changes into an adult.

segment
A part of something—for example, a worm.

shimmer
To sparkle and shine.

thorax
The middle part of an insect's body in between the head and abdomen.

tropical
A part of the world that has very hot, dry weather.

venom
Poison.

worker
A female honeybee or ant.

Index